Navigating the World of Road Racing:
A Beginner's Guide to Autocross, Track Days, and Road Racing

2nd Edition, 2024

Baez Racing Motorsports, LLC
(518) RACE-CAR
www.baezracingmotorsports.com
info@baezracingmotorsports.com

FOREWORD

Motorsports, in all its exhilarating forms, has always been a blend of precision, passion, and performance. From the adrenaline rush of autocross to the strategic intensity of road racing, the world of motorsports offers something for everyone—from novices testing their limits to seasoned drivers mastering the intricacies of the track.

This guide, Navigating the World of Road Racing: A Beginner's Guide to Autocross, Track Days, and Road Racing, serves as an invaluable resource for anyone looking to embark on this thrilling journey. Whether you're drawn to the accessibility of autocross, the learning opportunities in high-performance driving events (HPDE), or the full commitment required for road racing, this book lays out the essentials with clarity and depth.

Baez Racing Motorsports has crafted this guide not only to introduce you to the fundamentals of each racing discipline but also to provide practical advice on car preparation, safety requirements, and the often-overlooked elements of racing etiquette and track day preparation. The detailed insights into budget considerations, vehicle selection, and the progressive path from casual track days to competitive racing are particularly valuable for those new to the sport.

As you turn these pages, you'll find the tools and knowledge necessary to navigate your way through the exhilarating and demanding world of road racing. This guide is more than just a manual; it's an invitation to join a community of passionate individuals who share a love for speed, precision, and the relentless pursuit of perfection.

Whether you're here to pursue a lifelong passion or to simply experience the thrill of driving at the limit, may this guide inspire and equip you for the road ahead. Welcome to the world of motorsports—where every corner, every straight, and every lap brings a new challenge and a new story to tell.

— Joel Baez

CEO of Baez Racing Motorsports, LLC and Baez Motor Company, LLC

Table of Contents

1. **Chapter 1: This is me just thinking… What I want to do?** 7

2. **Chapter 2: Budget** 32

3. **Chapter 3: What car is best for me?** 56

4. **Chapter 4: Minimum requirements for a track day** 62

5. **Chapter 5: Minimum requirements for a Race Car** 68

6. **Chapter 6: Track Etiquette** 100

7. **Chapter 7: The Importance of Seat Time** 106

8. **Chapter 8: How Do I Get to the Next Level?** 110

9. **Chapter 9: What You Need to Know** 115

10. **Chapter 10: Getting More Involved** 120

11. **Glossary and Acronyms** 125

1. Chapter 1: Me just thinking… What I WANT to do?

It all started with a hum—a low, deep vibration that rumbled through my chest as I stood trackside at a local race event. The roar of engines, the smell of burning rubber, and the sheer adrenaline in the air were intoxicating. I watched as drivers navigated hairpin turns and blistering straights with surgical precision. At that moment, I knew this wasn't just a passing interest; it was a calling.

But where did I fit into this high-octane world? Could I see myself behind the wheel, pushing limits and chasing speed? Or was I content as a spectator, dreaming from the sidelines? These thoughts swirled in my mind, challenging me to dive deeper and explore what I really wanted out of life—and out of racing.

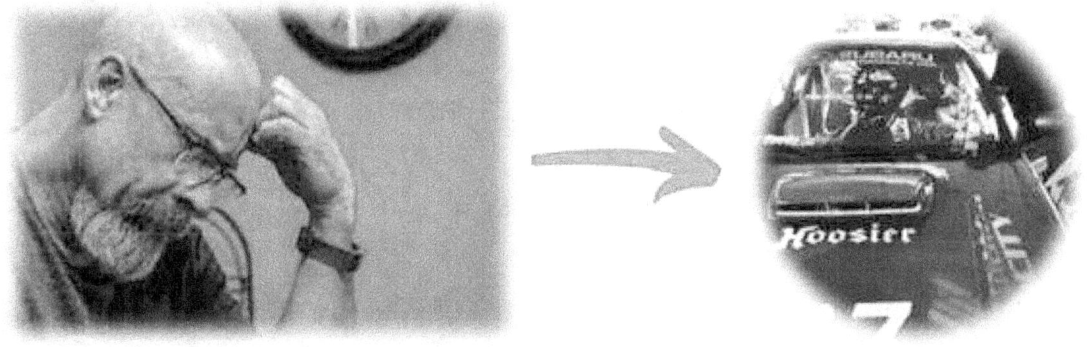

Road racing can be an exhilarating way to test your limits, both as a driver and as an enthusiast. The journey often starts with a simple thought: "What do I really want to do?" This chapter is about exploring that initial spark of curiosity and passion, digging into the reasons why you're drawn to the track, and understanding what it is you want to achieve in the world of road racing.

The first thing you need to determine is how much time and budget you can realistically dedicate to motorsport. This is a personal decision that varies greatly from one individual to another. Depending on your situation, you might find yourself able to spend every weekend at the track or only manage a single visit each year. This time commitment will influence your journey in motorsport, guiding you in choosing the right path and helping you assess your skills and position as a race car driver. It will also inform how much money it makes sense to invest in the sport.

In this guide, I will describe three of the most common track disciplines available at U.S. speedways, ranging from amateur to professional levels, all of which involve twisty road courses. The skills required to excel in road racing are quite different from those needed for other disciplines like oval racing, rally, drifting, or drag racing. The most popular road and track events are Autocross, Track Days, and Road Racing. Autocross is the entry-level discipline and the most affordable of the three. Track Days, or High-Performance Driving Events (HPDE), come next, requiring a bit more investment due to increased wear on your vehicle.

Finally, there's Road Racing, the most expensive and safety-intensive of these disciplines. That said, here are the differences and requirements for these three disciplines:

a. Autocross

Autocross, also known as Gymkhana, Autoslalom, Auto-X, or Solo (as it's often called), may seem simple on the surface. It typically involves setting up a mini-road course with traffic cones in a parking lot or other open space, where drivers compete to achieve the fastest time without hitting cones or going off course. Despite the relatively low speeds involved, Autocross is one of the most intense and fast-paced forms of motorsport you can experience. With low barriers to entry, it's an accessible way for many drivers to become competitive.

Autocross is also the most affordable form of motorsport. Competitors range from casual participants who drive the same car they use for their daily commute to dedicate enthusiasts with specialized competition cars, high-performance tires, and a commitment to fine-tuning every fraction of a second. Between these extremes, there are various levels and classes to accommodate different degrees of car modification. No matter your skill level or the car you drive, there's a place for you in Autocross.

What do I need?

✓ Your State Driver's License

Unless you're participating in one of the Karting classes, a current valid driver's license is required to enter an Autocross event. Make sure to bring it with you to show at registration. If you're under 18, both parents will need to sign a minor waiver for you to participate.

✓ Vehicle in Good Working Order

While Autocross doesn't require the same level of safety gear as other racing disciplines (though it is recommended), your vehicle must be in proper working condition. Ensure that all suspension parts are secure and not worn out, the car battery is firmly in place, tires are free from visible cords or metal, brakes and seatbelts are in good shape, and there are no fluid leaks. Additionally, a Snell-compliant helmet is required for almost all events. Before participating, a tech inspector will assess your car to ensure it meets all safety requirements.

✓ Helmet

A helmet is mandatory while driving on the course, though most events offer "loaner" helmets if you don't have your own. If you bring your own helmet, it must meet specific safety standards—more than just being "DOT-Approved." The most common certifications are Snell "M" and "SA," and the helmet should have a certification year of 2010 or later.

✓ Register

Some events require online registration in advance, while others allow on-site sign-up. When you find an event, be sure to check the registration details. Entry fees typically range from $250 to $400, depending on the racing club and whether it's a private or public event.

✓ Weather and Preparation

Autocross events proceed in all weather conditions—rain, shine, or even snow. Dress appropriately, wearing closed-toed shoes, and bring weather-appropriate gear, drinks, and snacks, as most tracks lack food services for smaller events like Autocross. Since loose objects are not allowed in your car while competing, it's a good idea to bring a plastic tote bin to store your belongings during the event.

✓ Pre-Event Preparation

Before heading to the tech inspection, make sure your car is emptied out. Open the hood and trunk for the inspectors. If you don't have pre-assigned numbers and the inspectors don't have shoe polish (usually white Griffin) to mark them on your window, ask for low-sticky painter's tape (blue tape) to create numbers and class letters.

✓ Technical Inspection

The technical safety inspection, known as "Tech," involves an auto-crosser inspecting your car to ensure it meets all safety requirements. They'll check under the hood, inside the interior and trunk, inspect the tires, verify that the suspension is secure, ensure your helmet is compliant, and confirm there are no loose parts in or on your car. The battery will also be checked, so make sure it's properly secured (no bungee cords).

✓ Walk the Course

Since you'll only get a few runs, it's crucial to walk the course beforehand and plan your approach. Arrive early enough to walk the course at least 2-3 times. Each walk typically takes 5-10 minutes depending on the location. The course should be marked well enough that you don't have to memorize it, but familiarizing yourself with it will usually improve your performance. Don't hesitate to ask an experienced participant for help if needed.

✓ Drive

This one is self-explanatory. After walking the course, head to the "grid" area where you'll park between runs. Grid workers will tell you when it's your turn to go up to the line for your run. Remember, the goal is to have fun, so focus on improving your time with each run, and most importantly, stay safe: safety always comes first.

✓ Progression in Autocross

Autocross offers various levels of competition, from schools that help you become a better driver to National Tours, National Championships, and even a Pro Series.

b. HPDE

The High-Performance Driving Event (HPDE) offers enthusiast drivers the opportunity to learn the nuances of high-performance driving on road courses in a safe and controlled environment.

These events are typically organized by sanctioned bodies such as SCCA, NASA, IMSA, FIA, or other event coordinators. During an HPDE, you'll be paired with an instructor who will sit in the passenger seat of your car, guiding you through every aspect of the experience. Your instructor will teach you the optimal driving line, the fundamentals of braking, precise steering inputs, and the importance of smoothness. You'll also learn to master the four key elements of every corner: finding the limit, utilizing the full width of the track, maximizing acceleration, and perfecting corner entry.

What do I need?

✓ Age and Licensing Requirements

Like Autocross, participants in HPDE (High-Performance Driving Events) must be at least 18 years old (or 16 with parental consent) and hold a current valid state driver's license. Your vehicle must meet the minimum technical requirements set by the sanctioning body, similar to those for Autocross. Additionally, it's essential to be familiar with and adhere to all applicable rules for your HPDE Group/Class, which can be found in the Club Codes of your Club Racing Program. By participating, you agree to always abide by these rules. Each driver must also be deemed physically fit by their physician to participate in this high-stress, physically demanding sport.

✓ Vehicle and Safety Inspection

Just like in Autocross, your car must undergo a technical inspection (tech) before being allowed on the track. It must pass this inspection to ensure it meets all safety standards. HPDE events, often referred to as "Track Days," allow you and your car to experience high-speed driving on a speedway in a safe and controlled environment. The focus is on learning the racing line, consistently hitting the apex, and improving lap after lap. The goal is not just speed but consistent performance. Becoming a fast driver comes with time, practice (seat-time), and, of course, talent!

✓ Minimum Attire

All participants must wear non-synthetic fabric clothing, such as cotton. While shorts are permitted, long pants are recommended, and closed-toe shoes are mandatory. In the pit lane, shorts are allowed except during sessions requiring refueling, such as endurance racing. Some racetracks may have stricter requirements, potentially prohibiting shorts and sleeveless shirts. A properly fitting helmet that meets Snell 2005 (SA2005; M2005) or ECE 22.05 standards, or newer (or equivalent), is required. Drivers should also wear eye protection like goggles, safety glasses, or face shields, preferably made from impact-resistant materials, especially when using an open-face helmet. Both the driver and any passengers must use modern, well-maintained stock seatbelts or a DOT-approved restraint system. Lap belts without shoulder restraints are not allowed.

✓ Registration

Some events require online registration before the event, while others allow you to sign up on-site. When you find an event, check the specific registration details. Entry fees typically range from $250 to $800, depending on the event, location, and whether it's a private or public event.

✓ Rules and Conduct

Each event has its own set of rules, and participants are expected to exercise common courtesy and good judgment. You are responsible for your conduct, as well as that of your guests, both on the track and in the paddock. Overly aggressive driving, risky passing attempts, or discourteous behavior can result in significant penalties. While on the track, all cars must have both front side windows completely open. Additionally, all occupants must always keep their hands and arms inside the car, except when using hand signals during HPDE sessions.

Hand Signals in HPDE

1. Slowing Down: When a driver is entering the pits or reducing speed below the normal track pace, they should signal by extending an arm vertically with their fingertips pointing towards the sky, if possible.

2. Passing Signals: To assist another driver in overtaking, hand signals should be used whenever possible. The driver should point to the side they wish to be passed on, ensuring the signal is visible to the overtaking driver.

3. Flag Station Acknowledgement: During the cool-down lap, all drivers should wave to acknowledge every manned turn station as a sign of respect and attention to the marshals.

Run Group Explanation

> ➢ Group One (HPDE 1): This is where you start. In HPDE 1, you receive 1-on-1 guidance from an experienced instructor who helps you learn to control both your car and your emotions. The instructor will teach you how to approach and navigate turns, determine the optimal gear, identify braking points, and execute proper exits. The session typically concludes with a lead-follow exercise. Passing is very limited in HPDE 1 and is only allowed in designated "Passing Zones."

> ➢ Group Two (HPDE 2): While still considered a novice, you've demonstrated to your instructor or stewards that you can drive solo. You must consistently and predictably apply the basic techniques learned in HPDE 1, always maintaining safety. Group 2 is often mixed with Group 1, offering additional seat-time for those who no longer need an instructor. The passing rules remain the same as in HPDE 1.

➢ Group Three (HPDE 3): The Intermediate Group. In HPDE 3, you've advanced to a higher level of high-performance driving. Passing rules are less strict, but passing is still only allowed with a "point by" or "wave by" from the car ahead. You'll also be permitted to pass in corners, requiring you to learn how to share the track at high speeds. Stewards closely monitor your behavior on the track in this group.

➢ Group Four (HPDE 4): Reserved for the most experienced drivers. In HPDE 4, there are no specific passing restrictions beyond using good judgment and adhering to road racing etiquette. This group allows you to fully enjoy the thrill of high-performance driving on a road track in a relatively safe and controlled environment. It's important to note that while HPDE involves high-speed driving, it is not door-to-door racing.

The Famous Passing Rules

> *No Passing in Restricted Zones:* Passing in "No Passing Areas," as defined by the Passing Rules (discussed at the drivers' meeting or provided with registration paperwork), is strictly prohibited. Each track has its own designated passing zones, usually located on straightaways where a "wave by" or "point by" is required from the car ahead. In advanced groups, there are generally no restrictions on passing zones, allowing passes in braking zones, corners, or straightaways—always with good judgment.

> *No Passing Under Yellow Flags:* Passing is prohibited under any yellow flag situation until the driver is past the incident or the next manned flag station that is not displaying a yellow flag.

> *Instructor "Wave By" Exceptions:* If an instructor driving a car waves a car by, it does not count as a pass. Drivers are not

allowed to pass under a yellow flag, even if they receive a "wave by" from another participant.

➢ *Mechanical Trouble Exceptions:* If a car is experiencing mechanical issues and is pulling off the track, a pass is allowed regardless of the passing rules.

➢ *No Passing in No Passing Zones:* A driver may not pass another driver in a no-passing zone or situation, even if the other driver waves them by.

➢ *Responsibility for Safe Passing:* The driver attempting a pass is solely responsible for ensuring the pass is executed safely. Drivers should ensure that the driver ahead is aware of the pass before attempting it.

In summary, HPDE is not racing; it's an opportunity to gain valuable seat-time and learn the techniques necessary to prepare for the next level. With experience, you can pursue a competition license and move on to Road Racing or competitive Time Trials (TT)/ Time Attack (TA). In TT/TA, drivers compete against the clock, with the fastest driver in each class winning the event. Most of the times the event is not door-to-door competition, but a test of individual skill and consistency in a predefined track.

c. Road Racing

The next level of competition and track experience is Road Racing, where a **deeper commitment is required**. To participate in a sanctioned club racing program, in most of the cases you'll need to fully dedicate yourself to at least three racing weekends. Additionally, you'll need specialized driver safety gear and a fully prepared race car to compete in these events. Before you can hit the track, you must acquire a competition license, which certifies that you are competent and safe enough to race alongside others.

Road Racing events offer the thrill of **wheel-to-wheel competition**. For local racers, regional racing provides an opportunity to compete against the best drivers in their area without the need to travel across the country. These events are filled with friendly competition and are an excellent way to gain experience and immerse yourself in the sport. Regions often collaborate to create divisional points championships, giving racers the chance to compete for a championship title without extensive travel.

In addition to regional events, there are National Championships, which allow drivers to compete across the entire United States throughout the racing season. These national events provide a platform for racers to test their skills against the top competitors in the country, offering an exciting and challenging experience that pushes drivers to their limits. Road Racing is where you can truly experience the excitement and adrenaline of wheel-to-wheel racing at its finest.

What I need?

✓ Racing License

Your journey in road racing begins with either a Provisional Racing License or a Novice Permit, depending on the racing club you join. Requirements vary between regions and clubs, so it's important to check their specific criteria. Once a driver has fulfilled all the requirements for a novice permit or provisional license—including obtaining the acknowledgment signature from the Race Director or

Chief Steward—they can be upgraded to a Full Competition License. Many clubs may also waive this requirement if you graduate from a reputable racing school, such as Skip Barber Racing School, Bertil Roos Racing School, or Pro Drive Racing School, among others.

✓ Driver Gear

Proper driver gear is essential for safety in road racing. This includes driving suits that cover the body from the neck to the ankles and wrists, with one-piece suits being highly recommended. All suits must bear an SFI 3.2A/1 or higher certification label or an FIA 1986 Standard or FIA Standard 8856-2000 homologation label. While fire-resistant underwear is optional with suits carrying these certifications, it's highly recommended for added protection. Helmets must be approved by the Snell Foundation with a Snell sticker from 2010 or later (SA2010/SAH2010, SA2015/SAH2015), the SFI (SFI Sticker SFI 31.1), or the FIA standard 8860-2004 or later, or the British Standards Institute (BS6658-85 type A/FR). Each helmet must be labeled with the driver's name.

The use of a certified **head and neck restraint system** (SFI 38.1 or FIA 8858-2002 or 8858-2010) is mandatory. Gloves made of leather or other fire-resistant materials without holes, fire-resistant socks, and face coverings (balaclavas) for drivers with facial hair are required. Hair protruding from beneath a helmet must be covered by fire-resistant material, which can also be achieved with a full helmet skirt. Goggles or face shields made of impact-resistant materials are recommended for drivers of open cars. Shoes must be made of leather or nonflammable material that covers the instep, with manufacturer ventilation pinholes allowed.

✓ Registration

Some events require online registration in advance, while others allow for on-site sign-up. It's important to check the details of each event for specific registration procedures. Entry fees can range from $250 to $3,000, depending on the event, location, and whether it's a private or public event.

✓ The Race Car

To compete in road racing, your car must be prepared according to the rule book and the class in which you'll be competing. At a minimum, all vehicles must meet the safety and equipment standards outlined in a **competition rules book** of the sanctioning body or club overseeing the event. Basic car requirements include a roll cage, competition seat, competition belts, a window net, and a fire extinguisher.

✓ Tires to the blacktop

As you reflect on your motivations and desires, it's crucial to keep an open mind. Road racing offers a wide array of paths, and understanding what drives you will help guide your decisions moving forward. Whether it's the thrill of speed, the pursuit of technical mastery, or the community of fellow racers, identifying your "why" is the first step on your journey.

Road Racing represents the pinnacle of amateur championship racing in North America, where the nation's best amateur drivers compete head-to-head. This is where start-to-finish, wheel-to-wheel action unfolds, and where drivers put not only their cars on the track but also their pride on the line. The spirit of camaraderie found here is fueled by adrenaline and passion, making road racing a true test of skill, determination, and emotion. This is where competition comes to life.

2. Chapter 2: Budget

I remember the day I sat down with a blank spreadsheet, staring at the vast emptiness that was supposed to hold the blueprint for my racing future. The excitement of hitting the track was tempered by the cold, hard reality of finances. I started penciling in numbers—costs for a car, track fees, safety gear, and those inevitable repairs.

As the columns filled up, the magnitude of my dream became clear. It was no longer just about passion; it was about practicality. I could still see the finish line, but the road to get there was paved with dollar signs. That first draft of my budget was like mapping out an uncharted course, one that required careful planning and a clear sense of direction. The challenge wasn't impossible, but it demanded a level of discipline and commitment I had yet to fully grasp.

Setting a budget is one of the most critical aspects of getting into road racing. Without a clear financial plan, your dreams of racing could quickly spiral into an unsustainable hobby. This chapter will guide you through the financial considerations, helping you balance your passion with practicality, ensuring you can enjoy the sport without breaking the bank.

What is the difference between track car and race car?

The distinction between a "track car" and a full "race car" lies in their level of modification, purpose, and adherence to specific racing regulations:

Track Car

✓ Purpose: A track car is typically a **modified street-car**, designed for use on a race track. It's often used for track days, driving schools, or non-competitive events. The modifications are focused on improving performance and safety while maintaining a level of comfort and reliability.

✓ Modifications: These can include upgraded brakes, suspension, tires, and sometimes engine tuning. Safety features like roll cages, racing seats, and harnesses may be added, but the car often retains some street-legal features, like a functioning interior and exhaust system.

✓ Regulations: Track cars do not necessarily adhere to a specific set of racing regulations. They are often built to meet the owner's preferences and the general requirements of track day events, which are usually less strict than formal racing rules.

✓ Street Legal: Some track cars may remain street legal, allowing them to be driven to and from the track.

Full Race Car

✓ Purpose: A full race car is **purpose-built** or extensively modified **solely for competitive racing**. These cars are designed to meet specific class or series regulations and are optimized for maximum performance within those rules.

✓ Modifications: Full race cars feature extensive modifications, including but not limited to, lightweight bodywork, aerodynamic enhancements, stripped interiors, racing-spec suspension, advanced engine tuning, racing slicks, and specialized safety equipment like full roll cages, fire suppression systems, and racing harnesses.

✓ Regulations: These cars must comply with the technical and safety regulations of a particular racing series or class (e.g., FIA, SCCA, IMSA). The modifications are typically constrained by the rules of the series, ensuring a level playing field among competitors.

✓ Street Legal: Full race cars are generally not street legal due to their extreme modifications, lack of necessary street equipment (like headlights, indicators, or emissions controls), and focus on track performance.

In summary, a track car is a more flexible, often dual-purpose vehicle used for non-competitive driving, while a full race car is a specialized, non-street-legal machine built for the rigors of competitive racing.

➤ Should I use my daily driver?

If you've decided to pursue Autocross or HPDE as your motorsport discipline, using your daily driver can be a practical and enjoyable option for track events. If your car is well-maintained and you upgrade your brake fluid to a high-temperature grade, you should have no trouble having fun on the track. This approach is particularly suitable if you visit the track occasionally—once or twice a year, or even quarterly (if you're willing to take some risks with your engine).

"Tracking" your daily driver means pushing your car to its performance limits, trying to shave off seconds with each lap. This will involve running the engine near it redline for extended periods, intense braking, significant stress on the suspension, and substantial wear on tires and braking systems (pads and rotors). The clutch and transmission will also face increased heat and stress. Remember, your lap times will improve with more track experience, so if you're only hitting the track a couple of times a year and don't aspire to become a road racing driver, it makes sense to use your daily driver.

To ensure your car remains in good condition for daily use, consider investing in a set of dedicated track tires, racing brake pads (safety is always the top priority), and replace fluids before and after each track event. This will help keep your car "fresh" for everyday driving. Alternatively, you could build a dedicated race car, which, while more expensive, will provide peace of mind and better performance on the track.

Here's a rough estimate of the costs involved:

- ✓ Racing Brake Fluid (including the initial flush) = $60-90
- ✓ Maintenance = $20-30
- ✓ Engine Oil (assume 5L capacity) ≈ approx. $80 plus Oil Filter and metal gasket; around $100 total

- ✓ Brake Pads:

    - ○ Front = $200-400

    - ○ Rear = $150-300

- ✓ Cooling: Replace coolant/antifreeze with water and Water Wetter® approx. $40

- ✓ Tires: $1,200-1,800 per set of 4

- ✓ Approximate Investment: $1,770 – $2,760

- ➤ My Race Car Project: Should I buy used or new?

The decision to buy a used or new car for your race car project depends largely on your budget and is a very personal preference. A commonly heard phrase in the racing community is: "Get someone else's project, and now it's your headache." This is partly true. A used car will generally be cheaper and may come with modifications or even as a fully prepped race car (**turn-key ready**), costing anywhere from the crazy range from cheap $5,000 (lemon) to $140,000 (exclusive exotic) depending on the class and condition. This option can be a double-edged sword—it can either save you money or introduce unforeseen issues.

Building a car from scratch is often more expensive, but the journey of building your race car is rewarding. You'll know your car inside and out, and the satisfaction of having built it with your own hands is priceless. On the other hand, purchasing a used car allows you to leverage existing components, save money, and focus on fine-tuning the car for performance and safety.

For amateur road racing, HPDE, or Autocross, unless you have a large budget, it doesn't make sense to buy a brand-new car for the track. Track cars endure heavy wear from debris, collisions, and the intense demands on the engine, transmission, suspension, and brake systems. Interior luxuries, air conditioning, and other non-essential components will need to be removed for safety reasons and to reduce weight. If you do buy new, it's better to start with a white body shell (sold by many manufacturers for racing purposes) and build the car according to your class specifications.

Keep in mind that amateur racing typically doesn't offer financial rewards, so it's important to budget **wisely**. A basic budget for components and equipment for a race car typically starts around $5,000 to $10,000, not including the cost of the car itself. This amount will increase depending on the quality of the parts you choose—the better the components, the higher the cost.

➢ Modifications

People attend racetrack events for **two primary reasons**: to have fun or to compete. In either case, you'll need to make some basic modifications to your car to improve safety and performance. These modifications can be categorized into essentials and nice-to-haves, depending on your goals and budget. Here's a breakdown of what you'll need, and the approximate costs associated with them for a Street Touring or Super Touring (ST) car:

Essential Modifications (Must-Haves)

- ✓ Racing Brake Pads and Fluid - Improves stopping power and resists fade under high temperatures.

- ✓ High-Performance Tires - Provides better grip and handling on the track.

- ✓ Suspension Upgrades - Enhances stability and cornering performance.

- ✓ Roll Cage (for higher levels of competition) - Essential for safety in case of a rollover.

- ✓ Racing Seat and Harness - Keeps you securely in place during aggressive driving.

Nice-to-Have (NTH) Modifications

- ✓ Engine Upgrades - Improves power output but may increase strain on other components.

✓ Cooling System Enhancements - Helps manage heat buildup, particularly in high-stress situations.

✓ Aerodynamic Upgrades (e.g., spoilers, splitters) - Enhances downforce and stability at high speeds.

✓ Weight Reduction - Removing non-essential components to reduce overall weight and improve performance.

The cost of these modifications can vary widely based on the quality of parts and the specific requirements of your racing class. Investing in the right modifications will make your car safer, faster, and more enjoyable to drive on the track.

Safety Equipment

Part	Average cost for a ST car	
	Track Car	Race Car
Roll Cage	No need it, but nice to have	Required: $3500
Race Seat	No need it, but nice to have	Required: $600
Race Net	Not applicable	Required: $60
Roll Cage Net	Not applicable	Required: $120
Roll Cage Padding	Not applicable	Required: $30
Racing Seat Belts	No need it, but nice to have	Required: $450
Kill Switch	No need it, but nice to have	Required: $100
Mirror Roll Cage	Not applicable	No need it, but nice to have: $90
Mirror Side Roll Cage	Not applicable	No need it, but nice to have: $75
Fuel Sample	Not applicable	Required: $140

Part	Average cost for a ST car	
	Track Car	Race Car
Fire Suppression	No need it, but nice to have	Required: $500
Radio Communications	Not applicable	No need it, but nice to have: $1,500
Towing Hooks	No need it, but nice to have	Required: $70
Racing Wheel with quick release	Not applicable	No need it, but nice to have: $600
Long Studs	No need it, but nice to have	No need it, but nice to have: $150
Racing Wheel Nuts	No need it, but nice to have	No need it, but nice to have: $180
Rain Light	Not applicable	Required: $120
Stainless Steel Brake Lines	Required: $200	Required: $200
Total	Required $200 / NTH $5,585*	Required $6,220 / NTH $8,565

*Estimate cost based on "*good*" performance parts, not "Race Car" quality.

Performance

Part	Average cost for a ST car	
	Track Car	Race Car
Wheels	No need it, but nice to have	$2,600
Wheel Spacers with hub	No need it, but nice to have	$450
Tires	$1,000	$1,700
Brake Pads	$250	$500
Rotors	No need it, but nice to have	$5,500
Brake Ducts	No need it, but nice to have	$350
Exhaust System (N/A)	No need it, but nice to have	$900
Exhaust System (Turbo)	No need it, but nice to have	$1,500
Intake (N/A)	No need it, but nice to have	$60
Intake and Intercooler	No need it, but nice to have	$1,500
Oil Cooling	No need it, but nice to have	$150
Radiator	No need it, but nice to have	$400
Clutch kit	No need it, but nice to have	$1,400
Flywheel	No need it, but nice to have	$250
Stainless Steel Lines (Power steering, clutch)	No need it, but nice to have	$100
Driveshaft (if applicable)	No need it, but nice to have	$1,300

Part	Average cost for a ST car	
	Track Car	Race Car
One Turn Power Steering Pump	No need it, but nice to have	$600
Dry Sump or Accumulator	No need it, but nice to have	$400
Catch Can or Air-Oil-Separator	No need it, but nice to have	$450
Short Shifter	No need it, but nice to have	$250
Ignition Coils	No need it, but nice to have	$100
Performance Spark Plugs	No need it, but nice to have	$50
Suspension System	$1,400	$3,500
Sway Bars and bushings	$900	$2,500
Aero	No need it, but nice to have	$2,00
Engine Internals (Long Block)	No need it, but nice to have	$9,500
Ancillary Engine Parts (Harmonic Balancer, EBC, MAF, Boost Controller, Etc.)	No need it, but nice to have	$3,500
Gauges	No need it, but nice to have	$600
Switches	No need it, but nice to have	$70
Fuel Pump	No need it, but nice to have	$150
Injectors	No need it, but nice to have	$1,300
Turbocharger System (if applicable)	No need it, but nice to have	$2,500
Transmission Internals	No need it, but nice to have	$4,500
Differential Internals (AWD/RWD)	No need it, but nice to have	$2,300
Silicone Hoses	No need it, but nice to have	$350
Hardware and clamps	No need it, but nice to have	$250
Transponder	Not Required	$300
Fuel Cell	Not Required	$500
Wipers	No need it, but nice to have	$25
Tuning	No need it, but nice to have	$600
Corner Balance	Not Required	$600
Stand Alone ECU	No need it, but nice to have	$2,500
Total	Required $3,700 / NTH $25,200*	$54,500

*Estimate cost base on "good" performance parts, not "Race Car" quality.

Yes, these prices are pretty accurate as of 2024, and it's clear that

racing and competition remain costly endeavors. When it comes to race cars, especially those built for amateur competition, the expenses can be significant due to the high-quality components and advanced engineering involved. This is why **professional race cars** now often command prices in the range of $400,000 to $450,000.

There are several websites where you can compare prices and assess the costs of both new and used race cars. Given the increasing investment required to build a race car from the ground up, it often makes more financial sense in 2024 to purchase a used race car and focus on debugging and refining it to suit your needs. By choosing a used race car, you can benefit from existing modifications and avoid the substantial costs and time commitment associated with a complete build, while still achieving competitive performance on the track.

➢ Towing and Storage

Towing a race car is an important cost to consider, especially since most race cars are not street-legal due to modifications to the suspension and exhaust systems, which are prohibited in many states. You'll also need a towing vehicle with a capacity of at least 5,500 lbs. While you could drive your track car to the event, this exposes the engine to potential overheating before you even reach the track. Additionally, unforeseen events—such as engine failure, a broken suspension, transmission issues, or brake line damage— might require you to tow your vehicle in a track day event. Towing services typically cost between $0.25 – $0.50 per mile, so for a local track, a round-trip tow could cost around **$600-800 per event**.

Another hidden cost of owning a race car is storage. If you don't have your own garage or warehouse, renting a storage space can add up. Depending on the size and exclusivity of the storage facility, along with any additional services provided (such as repairs or maintenance), you could be paying between **$700 - $900 per month**. Keep in mind that the <u>average hourly rate for a race car mechanic</u> is now around **$150-180**. These costs can quickly add up, so it's crucial to consider how reliable you want your car to be and the quality of the components you use.

One cost-effective alternative is to hire a track service company that provides comprehensive support at a fraction of the individual costs. These companies typically offer:

- ✓ Transportation of your vehicle to and from the track

- ✓ Pre-race and track preparation support, including:

- ✓ Assisting with driver setup (e.g., buckling in)

- ✓ Checking communication systems

- ✓ Inspecting the car before and after each session (e.g., tire temperature, pressure, and checking for leaks)

- ✓ Addressing any issues that arise during the event (e.g., worn belts, seized bearings, electronic malfunctions)

- ✓ Transponder rental (for competition purposes)

- ✓ Radio communications (if not already equipped)

- ✓ Coaching and mentoring to improve your racing line and overall performance

These services typically cost between **$2,800 - $3,500** per event.

If you need additional help on a track day, renting a uniform and helmet can cost around $100-120 per day.

Some track support companies offer more comprehensive packages, which may include:

- ✓ Entry fees

- ✓ Vehicle rental (race car)

- ✓ Hotel accommodations

- ✓ Meals (e.g., lunch)

These all-inclusive contracts can range from **$5,500 to $8,500** per event.

➢ Entry Fees

Entry fees for events vary depending on the sanctioning body, region, and event type. Here are the typical costs for 2024:

- Regional Event: $300 - $400

- National Event: $700 - $900

- US Championship Event: $1,400 – $1,700

- Track Day or Autocross: $200 - $300

- Time Trial Event: $300 - $400

A typical regional racing season, which consists of 6-8 events per year, will cost approximately $1,800 – $3,200 per season, just in registration.

Private racing clubs, which often compete for monetary prizes, have significantly higher fees. Costs can range from **$2,000 to $6,500** depending on the exclusivity of the club and the event. Private track days are also available and often involve dividing the cost of renting the track among participants, covering amenities, track workers, and medical personnel.

➢ Upgrading to Semi-Pro or Pro Racing?

Moving into Semi-Pro or Pro racing introduces a new level of financial commitment. As now, in 2024 season, you should budget between **$120,000 – $350,000**, depending on the class and sanctioning body (e.g., FIA, SCCA-Pro, IMSA, SRO). This budget includes entry fees but does not cover the cost of the race car or Time Attack car, fuel, tires, brakes, or spare parts. Additionally, racing at this level often requires traveling across the country to meet championship requirements and accumulate points. Therefore, you must also factor in the cost of accommodations (hotel or RV), state-to-state transportation, and towing for your car, tools, and equipment.

➢ Consumables

Identify the consumables on a race car, is pretty easy. Those are the components that wear due to use on a race or track event. The consumables required every single time at the track are:

✓ Fuel (Gasoline or Ethanol, if permitted)

✓ Engine Oil

✓ Oil filter

✓ Distilled Water

✓ Battery Charge (for those using EV's)

✓ The second group of most frequent consumables that you need to be on top of them are:

✓ Brake Pads

✓ Brake Fluid

✓ Tires

The next group of components that require keep an eye during maintenance are:

- ✓ Air filter
- ✓ Gear Oil
- ✓ Synchro and Differential Fluid
- ✓ Power Steering Fluid
- ✓ Spark Plugs

After every race or track event, it's recommended to at least replace the engine oil and filter. Also, it's recommended to flush the brake fluid every other race or weekend event. Also, you will need to replace the transmission oil and differential at least every three (3) events. All these recommendations are to keep your car in optimum conditions for the next season. Additionally, this minimize the cost of a failure since you are on top of the minimum maintenance required on the car. Overhaul of the engine should be done at the end of the season. Brake pads and rotors must be inspected at the end of each race weekend or track event and replace as needed it. Tires replacement depends on your driving style, your tire management strategy, and the length of the events. Also, the type of compound of the tire that you are using dictates the frequency how often you should replace them. Safety is your number 1 priority. Therefore, old tires, flat spots or worn tires may cost you more than a lot, they may cost your life. So, these should be inspected, at the end of each session. Sometimes, you catch bolts or sharp debris from the track, or you just simply overdrove the car and now you have expose wires. Tires are tricky, so monitor the temperature and pressure going out and coming in its so important to maximize the usage life of the racing tires.

With a well-planned budget, you're not just preparing yourself financially; you're also setting the stage for a sustainable and enjoyable racing experience. A clear understanding of your financial limits allows you to make informed decisions, ensuring that your journey into road racing remains both fun and financially manageable.

3. <u>Chapter 3: What car is best for me?</u>

The search for the perfect car felt like searching for a soulmate—an experience filled with anticipation, excitement, and a fair share of doubt. I scoured forums, attended car meets, and spoke to seasoned racers, each conversation pulling me in different directions. Was I a vintage classic kind of racer, leaning toward the timeless lines of a Porsche 911, or was I more at home in a modern machine, where technology meets raw power? I pictured myself in various cars, hands gripping the wheel, foot poised over the throttle, but none of them felt quite right until I stumbled upon it—my car. It wasn't the flashiest or the fastest, but the moment I sat in the driver's seat, something clicked. The seat hugged me like an old friend, and I knew this was the car that would take me where I wanted to go. It was as if the car chose me as much as I chose it, and from that moment on, we were in it together, ready to take on whatever the track had in store.

Choosing the right car is a pivotal decision in road racing. It's not just about finding the fastest or most powerful vehicle—it's about finding the car that fits your goals, experience level, and budget. In this chapter, we'll explore how to select the car that aligns with your aspirations and helps you make the most of your time on the track.

The type of daily driver you have or the cars you've driven can influence your proficiency with different engine and drivetrain configurations. Additionally, whether you opt for a track car, or a race car depends largely on your budget. The most common configurations include examples below:

- Front Engine with Front-Wheel Drive (FWD)

    o Honda Civic, Acura Integra

- Front Engine with Rear-Wheel Drive (RWD)

    o Mazda Miata, Chevrolet Corvette

- Front Engine with All-Wheel Drive (AWD)

    o Subaru WRX, Mitsubishi Evolution

- Mid-Engine with Rear-Wheel Drive (RWD)

    o Lotus Elise, Acura NSX

- Rear Engine with Rear-Wheel Drive/All-Wheel Drive

    o Porsche 911

- Mid-Engine with All-Wheel Drive (AWD)

    o McLaren 720, Lamborghini Huracan

Each configuration has its own set of advantages and disadvantages, which can vary depending on the track layout and weather conditions. Rear-wheel drive (RWD) is generally the easiest to manage on the track, providing a good balance of performance and control. All-wheel drive (AWD) tends to understeer but excels in icy or wet conditions, offering superior traction. Mid-engine setups are the most technical to drive and, in the hands of a skilled driver, can be the most effective on the track. However, these configurations also tend to be more expensive.

Front-wheel drive (FWD) is competitive and cost-effective, as long as the axles are well-maintained. Front-engine, rear-drive cars (RWD) are generally cheaper to maintain and can be very fast if well-balanced, though they may be prone to oversteer. Ultimately, the best configuration for you depends on your skill set and driving style.

When choosing the optimal engine and drivetrain configuration for road racing, several factors must be considered. These include the specific requirements of the race series or class, the weight and aerodynamics of the vehicle, and the engine's power and torque output.

In road racing, engine and drivetrain configurations typically prioritize power, torque, and reliability over fuel efficiency and emissions. Depending on the race series, this could mean using a high-performance engine with large displacement and high horsepower, paired with a robust and reliable transmission and drivetrain.

For example, some race series may require the use of specific engine types, such as a naturally aspirated V8 or a turbocharged inline four-cylinder. In other cases, teams may have more flexibility to choose the engine that best suits their vehicle's needs.

Ultimately, the ideal engine and drivetrain configuration for road racing will depend on the specific requirements of the race series, as well as the team's goals and capabilities. You know better than anyone what suits you best and what makes you feel safe on the track.

The car you choose will become your partner on this journey, so take the time to make an informed decision. By considering your goals and aligning them with the right vehicle, you're setting yourself up for success on the track, ensuring that every lap is a step closer to achieving your racing dreams.

4. Chapter 4: Minimum requirements for a track day

The night before my first track day felt like the calm before a storm.

My garage was a flurry of activity—tools scattered, tires stacked,

and a checklist pinned to the wall with items methodically crossed

off. I'd read the forums, watched countless videos, and absorbed

every piece of advice I could get my hands on. But standing there,

helmet in hand, it dawned on me that preparation wasn't just

about having the right gear—it was about mindset. I was about to take my car, a machine that had become an extension of myself, onto a track where the only thing separating me from the asphalt was my skill and judgment. The stakes felt high, but with each step of preparation, from checking tire pressure to packing my racing suit, the nerves transformed into a quiet confidence. I was ready, and as I loaded my car onto the trailer, I knew I had done everything possible to make this first experience on the track one to remember. Before hitting the track, it's essential to understand the minimum requirements needed to participate in a track day. This chapter covers the basic gear, car modifications, and safety checks you need to meet the standard regulations, ensuring that you're well-prepared for your first time on the track.

Requirements for Participating in a Track Day (Autocross or HPDE)

- ✓ Age Requirement

  - o Participants must be at least 18 years old, or 16 years old with parental consent.

- ✓ Driver's License

  - o You must hold a current, valid state driver's license.

- ✓ Vehicle Requirements

  - o You must have access to an automobile that meets the technical requirements and passes the tech inspection.

- ✓ Membership

  - o A current membership with a sanctioned body or car club is required.

- ✓ Safety Equipment

  - o Proper safety equipment must be used as per the applicable group or series rules.

- ✓ Fees

  - o All applicable fees must be fully paid.

- ✓ Rules and Regulations

  - o Participants must be familiar with all applicable rules found in the Club Codes and Regulations and fully agree to always abide by them.

✓ Physical Fitness

- o You must be deemed physically fit by a physician to participate in a high-stress and physically demanding sport like auto racing.

✓ Waivers

- o All required waivers, especially the "gate waiver," must be signed before entering the facility.

Paddock Rules

✓ Supervision

- o Children must always remain under close adult supervision due to the risk of severe injury or death in the event of an accident.

✓ Speed Limit

- o The speed limit in the paddock is 5 MPH for all vehicles except emergency vehicles. This applies to all motorized and non-motorized vehicles, including those of guests.

✓ Utilities

  - Oil, water, electrical power, and compressed air are the responsibility of the participant. All compressed air bottles or gas cylinders with a pressure exceeding 200 PSI must be securely fastened vertically or fully enclosed in a structure such as a rollaway or crash cart. If a cylinder is not secured upright or enclosed, a protective cage or cap must be placed around the cylinder's head.

✓ Fueling

  - Assume that fuel may not be available at the track unless otherwise stated in the registration email or drivers' meeting. Always bring your own fuel. Refueling should only be done in designated concrete areas or other open and ventilated areas. Participants must keep water on hand in the paddock in case of fuel spillage, as gasoline spills can damage the asphalt surface or make it slippery. If not washed away, the participant may be liable for repair costs, which can exceed $1,000.

✓ Jack Stands

- o Participants must bring boards to place under loaded jack stands to avoid damaging the asphalt surface at the track or racetrack garage.

✓ Trash Removal

- o Any leftover trash, vehicle body parts, tires, etc., must be removed from the facility by the participant.

✓ Parking

- o Proper parking is essential to ensure all participants fit into the paddock. Parking in fire lanes is strictly prohibited.

By adhering to these requirements, participants ensure a safe and compliant experience at the track.

With the right preparation, your first track day can be a thrilling and rewarding experience. Understanding and meeting the minimum requirements ensures not only your safety but also maximizes your enjoyment and learning on the track. Take these guidelines seriously, and you'll be ready to focus on the excitement of racing.

5. Chapter 5: Minimum requirements for a Race Car

Note: Assessment in this chapter is to compete in a Street Touring class or similar competitive class or group.

The transformation of my car from a street-legal vehicle to a race-ready machine was like watching a caterpillar become a butterfly—

albeit a very loud, very fast butterfly. I still remember the first time I drove it after the modifications. The harnesses strapped tightly, the roll cage gleaming under the garage lights, and the guttural growl of the engine as I turned the key. This wasn't just a car anymore; it was a purpose-built beast, designed to do one thing: race. Every bolt tightened, every fluid checked, every safety feature installed brought me closer to that first competitive race. But it wasn't just about the car—it was about the transformation in me, too. I wasn't just a driver anymore; I was a racer. And when I finally rolled onto the track, there was no turning back. This car, this machine, was ready to race, and so was I.

When stepping up from track days to competitive racing, your car needs to meet more stringent requirements. This chapter outlines the essential modifications and safety features necessary to transform your vehicle into a race-ready machine, compliant with racing standards and regulations.

✓ Fire Safety Requirements

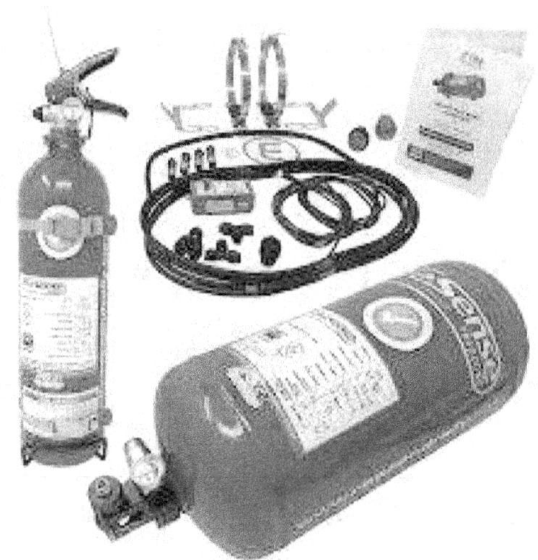

- Fire Extinguisher

All cars without an onboard fire suppression system must have a fire extinguisher securely mounted inside the vehicle within the driver's reach while seated with seat belts fastened and the steering wheel in place. The bracket must be metal with a quick-release type, and the mounting hardware must use a nut and bolt system—no sheet metal screws allowed. Fire extinguisher bottles made of plastic or aerosol-type cans are prohibited.

> Allowed Chemicals:

- Halon 1301, 1211, or Halotron I

- Hexafluoropropane, HFC-236a, CC0610, FE-36 (minimum 2 pounds)

- ABC dry chemical (minimum 2 pounds)

- 10BC potassium bicarbonate (Purple K) or sodium bicarbonate

- 1A10BC multipurpose ammonium phosphate and barium sulfate or Monnex

All fire extinguishers should have a gauge indicating their charge status. Bottles without a gauge should be weighed to determine content. **<u>Any bottle that has been discharged, even slightly, must be replaced or refilled</u>**.

- Fire Suppression System:

It is **highly recommended**, and required in some classes, **to have an onboard fire suppression system** in addition to a securely mounted fire extinguisher. An onboard system typically uses lines routed through the car with a single actuator to engage in case of emergency.

➢ Allowed Agents:

- Novec 1230, Halon 1301, 1211, or Halotron I

- Hexafluoropropane, HFC-236a, CC0610, FE-36 (minimum 5 pounds)

- AFFF material (e.g., SPA Lite, ZERO 2000, Coldfire 302) (minimum 2.25 liters)

- Lifeline Zero 360 Novec (2.25 liters or larger)

The system **must include a minimum of two nozzles**: one in the cockpit and one in the engine bay, with either manual or automatic release. All AFFF system bottles must have a working pressure gauge, and all bottles should be securely mounted with bolts. Systems may also use CEA614, provided that lines and nozzles are replaced according to the manufacturer's instructions. If an electric solenoid or switch is used to activate the fire suppression system, it should not lose power when the electrical master switch or vehicle ignition switch is turned off.

✓ Fire Extinguisher/Fire System Required Decal

Vehicles equipped with a fire extinguisher or suppression system must display an "E" decal on the outside of the vehicle to identify the location of the fire extinguisher or fire suppression activation switch. This **decal should be placed near the entry point** where the extinguisher/system is most accessible from the outside. For vehicles with fire systems, one decal is required at the release switch or button, and another on the outside of the vehicle.

✓ Fuel Cell Requirements

All cars must be equipped with an accessible **sampling port/valve/device** in the fuel line between the fuel tank or fuel cell and the carburetors or fuel injection system (or in an unused carburetor port) to allow safe acquisition of a fuel sample. The sampling port should be located outside the engine compartment if possible. The competitor is responsible for obtaining the sample without fuel leaking, spraying, or squirting.

- Fuel Cell/Tank:

When using a fuel cell, it must be FIA FT3 (or higher) certified. A fuel cell is required only if specified by class rules, but all vehicles with a fuel cell must comply with the rules and requirements of the sanctioned body, even if the fuel cell is not mandated by the class.

- Fuel Cell Recommendations:

  - A solid bulkhead should separate the fuel tank, fuel pump, fuel cell, filler neck hoses, and vent lines from the driver compartment.

  - The cell must contain a bladder that is FIA FT-3 (or higher) rated.

  - The cell should be in a container made of at least 0.036-inch steel, 0.059-inch aluminum, or 0.125-inch Marlex (crystalline polypropylene or high-density polyethylene), fully surrounding the bladder.

  - Internal foam baffling should be installed as per FIA FT3-1999 (or higher).

- ➢ The filler cap, line, and vent hoses should be designed to prevent fuel from escaping if the car is partially or fully inverted.

- ➢ A small drain hole in the outer box may be used to purge fuel trapped between the bladder and the box.

- ➢ The competitor is responsible for ensuring the cell, bladder, and components are installed, maintained, and replaced according to the manufacturer's instructions and in accordance with applicable sections of the rule book.

- ➢ The bladder must have a date of manufacture and serial number. The competitor is responsible for recording this information in the vehicle logbook. Bladders older than five years should not be used. Competitors must provide proof of the bladder's age. It is highly recommended that the receipt for the purchase of the bladder (or entire cell) be stored with the Vehicle Logbook.

> A single external container that fuel is stored in, or moves through (e.g., swirl pots, vent cans, surge tanks), may be used, provided it does not exceed 1.5 liters (0.4 gallons) in capacity and is constructed of metal with threaded fittings to stainless steel braided fuel hoses. The container must be separated from the driver's compartment by a bulkhead. Containers over 1.5 liters are considered additional fuel cells and must meet fuel cell requirements.

- Rotary-Molded Cells:

Rotary-molded cells are generally prohibited unless the bladder meets current FIA FT3 specifications and carries the appropriate certification mark, label, or stamp.

✓ Driver Restraint System

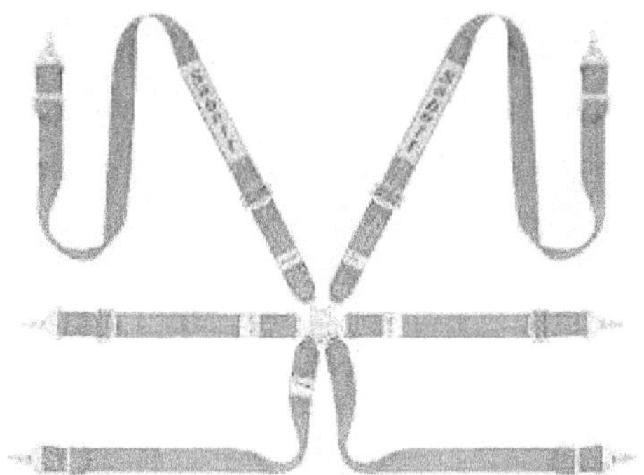

All vehicles must have a five (5), six (6), or seven (7) point **seat belt system.** Arm restraints are required in open cars and vehicles with open T-tops, Targa tops, missing or glass moon/sunroofs. A five-point system includes a lap belt, two shoulder belts, and an anti-submarine strap. A six-point system, recommended for upright or semi-reclining seating positions, adds a second anti-submarine belt. A seven-point system, recommended for seats with more than a 30-degree incline, adds additional support.

- Requirements:

All straps must be in new or perfect condition. Metal quick-release buckles with a **single point of release for all belts are required**. The shoulder harness should be mounted behind the driver at an angle between zero and twenty degrees from horizontal. The harness must be mounted to a specific guide bar or part of the chassis or cage—not to the seat. Only separate shoulder straps are permitted; "H" type belts are allowed, but "Y" type belts are prohibited. Each shoulder strap must have an independent mounting point, and all hardware must be SAE Grade 5 or better. Large diameter mounting washers should be used to distribute the load. Bolting through floor panels is prohibited without the required washers.

- Certification:

Belts must meet SFI Specification 16.1 or 16.5 with a dated label no more than two years old or showing an expiration date. Alternatively, FIA 8853/98, D-###.T/98, or higher certification is acceptable. FIA-certified belts have a label with an expiration date, and belts cannot be used past December 31st of the labeled year. Drivers are responsible for ensuring their belts are properly worn, adjusted, and latched. Any driver involved in a high-impact crash must send their belts to the manufacturer for inspection, re-webbing if necessary, and re-certification before reuse. Proof of re-certification is the driver's responsibility. All belts must be threaded according to the manufacturer's instructions.

✓ Roll Cage

The primary purpose of the roll cage is to protect the driver in the event of a rollover or collision. While chassis stiffening is a secondary benefit, it is not the primary intent of the rules. The cage may be removable or permanently welded, provided all aspects meet the sanctioned body's rules. **Any roll cage surfaces that may**

contact the driver's head, knees, or elbows must be padded with high-density padding, such as Ethafoam or Ensolite, designed for road racing use.

- Design Specifications:

Tubing must show no signs of crimping or wall failure, and all bends should be of the mandrel type with a center radius no less than three times the outside diameter of the tubing. The main roll cage hoop should be as wide as the interior and as close to the roof as possible, using a continuous length of tubing with no more than four bends totaling 180 degrees ± 10 degrees.

- Additional Requirements:

A diagonal brace must be used in the same plane as the main hoop, attaching to the corner above the driver's head and the opposite side's mounting plate. The forward hoops should extend from the main hoop to the floor, following the roof and "A" pillar. A connecting bar should link the forward hoops at the top of the windshield, as close to the roof as possible. Optional "Halo Hoop" or "Front Hoop" designs may also be acceptable.

- Rear Braces:

The main hoop should have two braces extending to the rear, attached as near to the top as possible, and without any bends. The rear braces should be mounted to the rear shock mounts or suspension pickup points, potentially passing through rear bulkheads, which must be sealed around the cage braces. Exceptions exist for cars with rear windows/bulkheads that prohibit rear brace installation.

- Door Bars:

At least two door bars are required on the driver's side and one on the passenger side. An "**X**" design counts as two bars. Modifications to non-chassis structures (door panels, inner door sheet metal, windows, door internals) may be made to accommodate door bars, but removal of material is limited to what is necessary to accommodate the bars. Door bars must not attach to the roll cage, and any modifications to the B-pillar for door bars must be minimal.

- Mounting Points:

The **roll cage must be mounted to the floor area**, including rocker panels, in six, seven, or eight points. The cage should not pass through the firewall. Plates or mounting boxes must be used at all attachment points, with each required cage bar terminating on a plate with a 360-degree weld. Only one mounting point per plate is allowed, and all additional tubes must be mounted as close to the required tube as possible.

- Plates:

Each mounting plate should not exceed 100 square inches or be less than nine square inches. Welded mounting plates should be at least 0.080 inches thick and may extend onto vertical sections of the structure.

- Bolt-In Cages:

Bolt-in cages must use reinforcing plates to sandwich the body, with **at least three bolts per plate**, and the plates must be at least $^3/_{16}$ inch thick. Hardware must be SAE Grade 5 or better, with a minimum of $^5/_{16}$ inch bolts. All **nuts must be securely held by a locking system** such as safety wire, lock washer, Nylock, or jam nuts. Nylock or crimping lock nuts must not be reused.

- Tubing:

Tubing must be welded 360 degrees around the circumference, and all tubes must meet minimum size and thickness specifications based on vehicle weight. Additional tubing can be of any size/dimension but must not create an unsafe situation. Roll cages must be inspected for quality welding, and any factory-installed cages may be permitted without 360-degree welds.

- Padding:

Any part of the cage that may come into contact with the driver must be padded with high-density padding designed for road racing. The padding must cover areas such as the head, knees, and elbows.

✓ Master Switch:

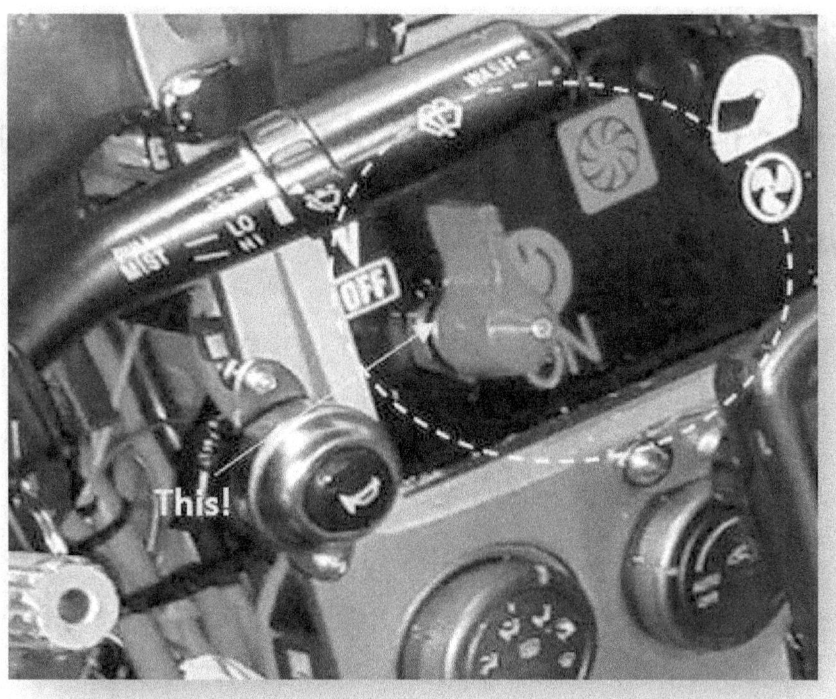

An electrical master switch is required and must be easily **accessible from outside** the vehicle. It should shut off the engine and cut all power, except for the onboard fire system, radio communication, and any other life support/medical device. The switch location must be clearly marked with a master switch cut-off decal.

✓ Steering Wheel Lock:

The steering wheel lock must be removed or disabled.

✓ Windows/Window Nets:

Vehicles must operate with <u>side glass windows fully open</u>. A **window net is required on the driver's side** and must be installed with a quick-release mechanism that allows it to fall toward the floor when released. Fasteners must be metal and attached to the roll cage. The window net must be **less than five years old**, carry an SFI or FIA label, and be in excellent condition. <u>Window safety nets are required on the driver's side window of all closed cars unless factory (OEM manufacturer) and FIA GT3/GT4 race-prepared cars with fixed Lexan front door windows.</u>

- ✓ Tow Eyes:

All race vehicles must have **at least two easily accessible tow eyes or tow points**, one in the front and one in the back. They must not protrude dangerously and should not require manipulation of bodywork or panels to access. The tow crew is not liable for any damage to your car if tow eyes or towing points are unavailable.

✓ Windshield/Sunroof Clips, Headlights:

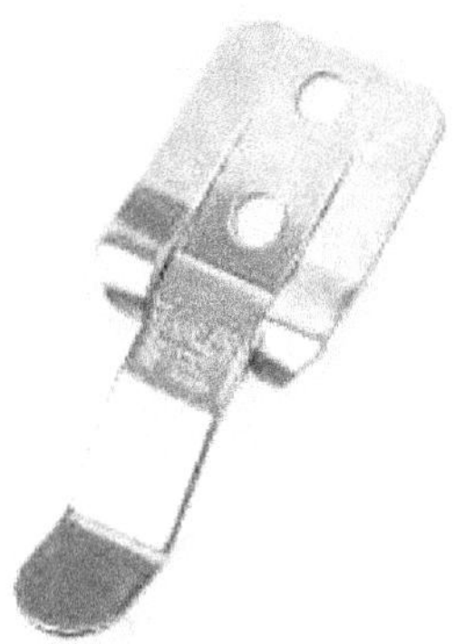

Windshield clips are recommended to prevent the windshield from ejecting in a crash. Sunroof clips are required, and glass sunroofs (moon roofs) must be removed or taped on both sides. <u>Headlights should be taped to protect them from rocks.</u> Polycarbonate windshields and rear windows securely bolted to the frame do not require clips or straps.

✓ Hoses Inside Cockpit:

All hoses carrying **flammable liquids or toxic gases** through the cockpit must be metal, steel-braided, or reinforced.

✓ Lights:

- Brake Lights: At least two working red brake lights must be visible from 300 feet to the rear. Certain race cars may be exempt at the discretion of the Event Director.

- Headlights: Not specifically required unless class/series rules specify.

✓ Driver's Seat:

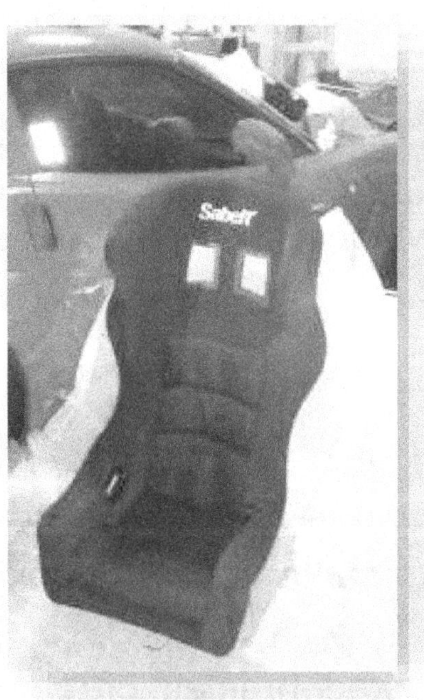

The driver's seat must be securely fastened and braced to minimize the risk of breaking loose during an impact. Large fender washers and solid fabricated mounts are recommended. **Seats made primarily of plastic, polymer, PVC, ABS, or similar materials are prohibited.** The installation must conform to all manufacturer requirements. The seat should be mounted to a steel floor pan with reinforcements or through a frame member. A **right-side impact head restraint system is required for all vehicles except formula cars.**

✓ Driver's Attire:

Drivers must wear a one-piece suit that covers the entire body except for hands, feet, and head. The suit must carry an SFI 3.2A/1 rating or higher (3.2A/5, 3.2A/10, 3.2A/15, or 3.2A/20) or FIA 8856-2000. Long underwear made of fire-resistant material must be worn with all suits except those rated 3.2A/5 or higher. Gloves made from fire-resistant material, shoes that fully cover the foot, and socks made of fire-resistant material are required. Helmets must be Snell SA2015, EA2016, or newer. A head and neck restraint system with an SFI 38.1, FIA 8858-2002, or FIA 8858-2010 certification label is mandatory.

✓ Engine Coolant:

Glycol-based antifreeze and other additives that may cause slippery conditions if spilled are prohibited. Other water additives, such as Redline Water Wetter, may be used.

✓ Alcohol Injection (where permitted by class rules):

Tanks containing alcohol exceeding 50% by volume must be FIA FT3 (or higher) rated and installed per fuel cell regulations. Tanks containing 50% or less alcohol by volume may use any container per the manufacturer's instructions but must be separated from the driver by a solid bulkhead or firewall.

✓ Ballast:

All ballast must be solid metal (e.g., steel, lead, or depleted uranium) and bolted in place with through-bolts, fender washers, and locking nuts. All hardware must be SAE Grade 5 or higher.

✓ Exhaust Exit:

The exhaust must exit behind and away from the driver's seat location.

✓ Fuel Caps:

Fuel caps must prevent fuel from spilling out of the tank during hard driving. Operational Monza-type caps are prohibited, though decorative covers are allowed.

✓ Rearview Mirrors:

The <u>vehicle must have at least one rearview mirror</u> that provides good visibility to the rear.

✓ Exposed Wires:

There should be no exposed wires inside the driver's compartment that could interfere with safe vehicle operation. No live wires may be exposed anywhere in the vehicle. <u>The battery must be securely fastened, with an electrically non-conductive material covering the positive terminal.</u> Batteries inside the driver's compartment must be fully covered and secured in a marine-type battery case. Lithium-ion batteries must be located outside the passenger area, as they pose a high fire risk if ruptured.

✓ Firewall and Floor:

The firewall and floor must prevent the passage of flame and debris into the driver's compartment. Belly pans should be vented to prevent liquid accumulation, and rear engine cars must have an undertray to protect the driver's legs and torso.

✓ Fuel:

Cars must use permitted fuel (gasoline or diesel) that meets dielectric constant standards and does not contain prohibited substances above specified limits. <u>Fuel must be free of additives that could cause slippery conditions if spilled on track.</u>

✓ Identification Markings:

The vehicle must display its assigned car number and class on both sides. Numbers and class letters must be legible and meet size requirements:

- 8 inches high for numbers

- 4 inches high for class letters

✓ Leakage and Caps:

There must be no visible fluid leaks on the vehicle.

✓ Loss of Bodywork:

All major body components must be maintained in their normal positions throughout competition. Loss of bodywork may result in a black flag, and finishing a race with missing bodywork may result in penalties.

✓ Oil Catch Tanks, Filters, and Breathers:

Oil catch tanks are required for engine breathers, transmission breathers, and any system venting fluids. The minimum capacity for catch tanks is **one U.S. quart**.

✓ Scatter Shields/Chain Guards:

Scatter shields or explosion-proof bell housings are required on cars where clutch or flywheel failure could pose a hazard. Chain drive cars must have protective cases/shields to retain the chain in case of failure.

✓ Steering Wheels:

<u>Wood-rim</u> steering wheels are prohibited.

✓ Suspension and Steering:

Suspension and steering components must be of suitable design and in good working order. Non-metallic suspension control arms, locating links, toe/steering links, and pushrods are prohibited unless specifically permitted.

✓ Tires:

<u>Tires must be DOT approved</u>, rated for at least 124 mph (U-rated) unless otherwise specified. Re-grooving of DOT tires is prohibited,

but grooving of non-DOT tires is permitted. Recapping of tires is not allowed.

- ✓ Tonneau and Boot Covers:

Tonneau covers and boot covers must be removed.

- ✓ Weight:

All cars must meet or exceed the minimum weight specified for their class with the driver, as weighed immediately after a race or qualifying session.

✓ Wheel Fans:

Wheel fans are permitted unless otherwise restricted by class rules.

✓ Wheel Rim Width:

Wheel rim width is measured at the base of the bead seat.

✓ Windows:

Windows must be clear or uncolored. Officials may require replacement of windshields deemed a safety hazard. Factory and FIA GT3/GT4 race-prepared cars with fixed Lexan front door windows may race as delivered. All other closed cars must run with both front door windows fully open.

This detailed summary provides a comprehensive overview of the requirements and recommendations for participating in a track day or HPDE event, ensuring clarity and safety for all participants.

Building a race car is an investment in both time and resources, but meeting the minimum requirements is crucial to ensure your safety and competitiveness on the track. By adhering to these standards, you're not just preparing your car for the race—you're also preparing yourself for the challenges and thrills that come with competitive racing.

6. <u>Chapter 6: Track Etiquette</u>

<u>On the track, respect isn't just earned through speed; it's earned through conduct</u>. My first track day taught me this lesson in spades. I'll never forget the moment a seasoned racer pulled me aside after a session. He wasn't angry, but there was a seriousness in his tone as he explained the importance of signaling before a pass and maintaining a predictable line. His words carried the weight of experience, and I realized then that track etiquette was more than just following rules—it was about **ensuring everyone's safety and maintaining the integrity of the sport**. The track isn't just a place to compete; it's a place to learn and grow as a community. That day, I became not just a better driver, but a more conscientious racer, understanding that how I acted on the track was as important as how fast I drove.

Good track etiquette is vital for ensuring a safe and enjoyable experience for everyone involved. This chapter dives into the unwritten rules of the road racing community, covering everything from passing protocols to communication on the track, helping you navigate the social aspects of racing with confidence.

Racing Room and Contact

Drivers are responsible for avoiding physical contact with other cars on the racetrack. Every competitor has the **right to racing room**, which is defined as sufficient space on the marked racing surface to maintain control of their car under racing conditions. Respecting this right is crucial. Abrupt changes in direction that impede or affect the path of another car attempting to overtake may be seen as an effort to deny another driver their right to racing room. **The overtaking driver is responsible for deciding when to pass and ensuring it is done safely. The overtaken driver must be aware of the passing attempt and avoid impeding or blocking the overtaking car.**

Stopping On Course

Stopping on the course is prohibited unless in the case of an emergency. "Stopping" includes sudden or unexpected slowing to a near stop. **Helping a disabled car is not allowed**. Emergencies for HPDE purposes include medical issues, mechanical failures that prevent pitting, onboard fires, or damage from an incident that renders the vehicle unfit to continue safely to the pits.

Emergency Stops

If you must stop in an emergency, your first concern should be **placing the car in a safe area** where it will not endanger other drivers. Never stop on the racing line, in a corner, or at an apex. When stopping off-course, avoid parking on dry grass or areas where a fire hazard might be posed due to exhaust temperature or leaks.

Counter-Course Driving

Driving against the normal traffic flow on the course is strictly prohibited except under these conditions:

- ✓ The track is closed, or the session has ended and been cleared.
- ✓ Ordered by an Emergency Response Team Official.
- ✓ In extreme emergencies, for a short distance, solely to get out of harm's way.
- ✓ Directed by a Marshal or Corner Worker.

Spins or Off-Track Excursions

If involved in a spin or off-track excursion, you must pull into the pits immediately after reentering the track. Officials will inspect the car and discuss the cause of the incident. If you spin off, seek assistance from a Course Official to wave you back on safely or signal for a tow.

Body Contact

__Body contact is strictly prohibited__ in any HPDE event. Anyone involved in contact must report immediately to the event Officials. Penalties, including possible permanent and immediate ejection from the event, will be enforced.

Post-Accident or Emergency Protocol

After an accident or rollover, drivers should remain in their vehicle (unless there is a fire, in which case they must exit safely) with seatbelts and helmets on until the Emergency Response Team arrives and clears them from the situation.

Post-Accident Reporting

All drivers involved in any significant accident or incident must report to the medical staff immediately for a check-up. Failure to do so may result in suspension from future events and could void personal medical insurance coverage. Significant accidents include:

- ✓ Any rollover, regardless of damage.

- ✓ Any impact rendering the vehicle inoperable.

By mastering track etiquette, you're contributing to a positive and respectful racing environment. These practices are essential not just for safety, but also for fostering a sense of camaraderie among racers. Understanding and adhering to these guidelines will help you earn the respect of your fellow racers and enhance your overall experience on the track.

7. Chapter 7: The Importance of Seat Time

In road racing, experience behind the wheel—commonly referred to as "seat time"—is invaluable. This chapter explores why spending as much time as possible on the track is crucial for improving your skills, building confidence, and truly mastering the art of racing.

There's a saying in racing: "You can't buy experience." It's a truth that hit me hard after countless hours on the track, chasing lap times and perfecting my technique. My first few sessions were a blur of adrenaline and nerves, each lap teaching me something new—how to brake later, how to find the perfect racing line, how to listen to my car's feedback. But with each passing hour, something shifted. The track started to feel less like a battleground and more like a familiar friend. Every corner, every straightaway became a lesson in control and confidence. It wasn't about mastering the track; it was about mastering myself, understanding my limits, and knowing when to push them. Seat time became my greatest teacher, and with each lap, I grew closer to the racer I aspired to be.

Seat time is crucial for any race car driver aiming to improve their skills and performance on the track. In this chapter, we'll explore why seat time is so important and how it can help you become a better driver.

Experience

Seat time refers to the amount of time a driver spends behind the wheel, including practice sessions, testing days, and actual racing events. The more seat time a driver accumulates, the more opportunities they have to hone their skills, become familiar with their car, and gain valuable experience. Experience is a key factor in racing success; the more time spent on the track, the better a driver will understand their car, the track, and the competition. This knowledge enables better decision-making, quicker reactions to situations, and ultimately, improved performance.

Muscle Memory and Reflexes

Racing is physically demanding, and repeated practice helps develop muscle memory and reflexes. These reflexes become crucial in high-pressure situations where split-second decisions are needed. The more seat time a driver has, the more instinctive and precise their reactions become.

Mental Development

Racing is not just **physically demanding**; it's **mentally exhausting** as well. Seat time helps drivers develop focus and concentration, especially during long races where maintaining mental sharpness is essential. The more time spent on the track, the better a driver can manage mental fatigue and maintain their concentration throughout the race.

Confidence Building

Confidence is a key factor in racing. The more time a driver spends behind the wheel, the more comfortable and confident they become. This confidence translates into better decision-making and, ultimately, improved performance on the track.

In conclusion, seat time is indispensable for any race car driver looking to enhance their skills and performance. It offers opportunities to gain experience, develop muscle memory and reflexes, improve mental focus, and build confidence. The more seat time a driver has, the better prepared they are to succeed on the track.

There's no substitute for experience, and the more seat time you accumulate, the more proficient you'll become. Consistent practice not only hones your technical skills but also deepens your understanding of your car and the track. Prioritizing seat time is essential for anyone serious about progressing in the world of road racing.

8. Chapter 8: How Do I Get to the Next Level?

Once you've got some experience under your belt, the question becomes: "How do I get to the next level?" This chapter delves into the strategies and steps you can take to elevate your racing game, whether that means competing in higher-level events, refining your techniques, or gaining more advanced skills.

Me at 1997. Let them start young!

There came a point in my racing journey when just showing up wasn't enough. I wanted more—I wanted to compete, to win, to be the best. But moving up to the next level wasn't just about being faster; it was about being smarter, more strategic. I remember watching the pros, their every move calculated, every decision deliberate. I studied their lines, their techniques, even their mental preparation. The next level was a different world, one where the margin for error was razor-thin and the competition fierce. I knew I had to step up my game, not just physically but mentally. It was no longer just about driving; it was about racing with purpose. Every practice, every race became a steppingstone toward that goal, each one teaching me something new about what it truly meant to be a top-tier racer.

Becoming a professional race car driver is a dream for many motorsports enthusiasts. It's a challenging and competitive field, but with hard work, dedication, and the right opportunities, you can turn your dream into reality. Here's a roadmap to help you on your journey to becoming a pro race car driver:

➢ Step 1: Start racing at a young age many professional race car drivers begin their careers early, often in karting or junior racing series. Starting young allows you to gain experience and build essential skills behind the wheel. It's also an opportunity to get noticed by teams and sponsors, as many professional drivers are scouted from these early stages.

➢ Step 2: Obtain the right education and training while experience on the track is crucial, a solid foundation in the technical aspects of racing is equally important. Understanding car mechanics, aerodynamics, and race strategy can give you an edge. Many racing schools and programs offer specialized education and training in these areas. Joining a racing team or program also provides hands-on experience and exposure to the racing industry.

➢ Step 3: Build a strong racing resume as you progress in your racing career, it's vital to build a strong resume that highlights your skills and achievements. Participate in as many racing events as possible and aim to perform well. Getting involved in testing and development programs can also make you stand out to potential teams and sponsors.

➤ Step 4: Network and make connections networking is crucial in the racing industry. Get to know team owners, engineers, and other drivers. Participate in racing organizations and events to meet and connect with industry professionals. Building a strong network can open doors to new opportunities and partnerships.

➤ Step 5: Seek sponsorship and funding racing at the professional level is expensive, and securing sponsorship is often essential. Start seeking sponsorship opportunities early in your career. Be proactive in reaching out to potential sponsors, create a compelling sponsorship proposal, and consider working with a marketing or sponsorship agency to enhance your efforts.

Becoming a professional race car driver requires a combination of hard work, dedication, and strategic planning. It's a challenging and competitive field, but with the right approach and a commitment to continuous learning and adaptation, you can achieve your dream.

Advancing to the next level in road racing requires dedication, strategy, and a willingness to continually learn and improve. By following the steps outlined in this chapter, you're positioning yourself to rise through the ranks and achieve greater success on the track, turning your racing dreams into reality. Good luck on your journey to becoming a pro race car driver!

9. Chapter 9: What You Need to Know

The first time I dove into the depths of racing knowledge, it felt like opening Pandora's box. There was so much more to road racing than I ever imagined—rules, regulations, technical jargon, and strategies that went far beyond just driving fast. I remember sitting down with a seasoned racer who had been in the game for decades. Over coffee, he walked me through the nuances of tire pressure, fuel management, and the physics of cornering. His stories weren't just lessons; they were insights into the mindset of a racer. Each piece of knowledge was like a tool, and the more I learned, the better equipped I became. Racing wasn't just about what happened on the track; it was about understanding the sport from every angle. The more I knew, the more confident I became, and the more I fell in love with the intricacies of racing.

There's a lot to learn when it comes to road racing, and this chapter is designed to equip you with the essential knowledge needed to navigate the complexities of the sport. From understanding racing jargon to grasping the rules and regulations, this chapter ensures you're well-prepared for all aspects of road racing.

If you're considering a career as a race car driver, there are several important factors to keep in mind:

- ✓ Physical Demands

  - ▪ Racing is a physically demanding sport. Drivers must maintain a high level of physical fitness to handle the intense G-forces, heat, and stress experienced on the track. Being in top physical condition is essential for optimal performance.

- ✓ Competitive Nature

  - ▪ The racing industry is highly competitive, with many aspiring drivers vying for limited opportunities. To succeed, you need to be proactive in seeking out opportunities, continuously improving your skills, and building a strong racing resume.

✓ Time and Dedication

- Racing is a full-time commitment. Drivers often spend long hours practicing, testing, and competing. It requires significant dedication and hard work to achieve success in this field.

✓ Financial Investment

- Racing at a professional level involves significant expenses, including equipment, travel, and entry fees. It's crucial to have a clear plan for funding your racing career, whether through sponsorship, personal investment, or other financing methods.

✓ Safety Risks

- Racing is inherently dangerous, with a risk of accidents and injuries. It's important to prioritize safety at all times and be prepared for the risks associated with the sport.

A career as a race car driver demands a strong commitment to the **physical, financial, and mental** challenges of the sport. While it's a demanding field, those who are dedicated and willing to work hard can find it to be a rewarding and exhilarating career.

Knowledge is power, and in road racing, being well-informed can make all the difference. By taking the time to learn the ins and outs of the sport, you're setting yourself up for a smoother, more successful racing journey. Use this knowledge as your foundation, and you'll be ready to tackle any challenge that comes your way.

10. Chapter 10: Getting More Involved

After years of racing, I started to realize that my passion extended beyond just driving. I found myself drawn to the community, the camaraderie, and the shared love of the sport. I began volunteering at events, helping organize track days, and even mentoring new drivers. It was during one of these volunteer days, watching the excitement in a novice driver's eyes as they prepared for their first track session, that I understood the true spirit of racing. It wasn't just about the thrill of the race; it was about being part of something bigger. The relationships I built, the knowledge I shared, and the experiences I gained from being more involved deepened my connection to the sport. Racing had given me so much, and now it was my turn to give back, helping to nurture the next generation of racers and ensuring the sport I loved continued to thrive. For those who want to go beyond just racing, there are many ways to get more involved in the road racing community. This chapter explores the different roles and opportunities available, from volunteering and networking to contributing to the sport in various capacities, allowing you to deepen your connection to the racing world.

If you're passionate about racing and want to get more involved in the industry, here are some ways to deepen your engagement:

- ✓ Join a Racing Team or Program
    - Many racing teams and programs offer opportunities for aspiring drivers to gain experience and develop their

skills. Whether it's karting, junior racing series, or more advanced programs, joining a team is a great way to get involved.

✓ Volunteer at Racing Events

- Racing events often need volunteers for tasks such as marshalling, scoring, or working in the pits. Volunteering is a great way to get close to the action, gain valuable experience, and make connections in the industry.

✓ Join a Racing Organization

- Joining a racing organization, such as a karting club or a sanctioning body, can provide access to racing events, resources, and networking opportunities. Being part of a racing community helps you stay connected and informed.

✓ Attend Racing Schools and Workshops

- Racing schools and workshops offer training in car mechanics, aerodynamics, race strategy, and other aspects of racing. These programs are valuable for learning more about the sport and connecting with industry professionals.

✓ Participate in Testing and Development

- Many racing teams and manufacturers offer testing and development programs for drivers. Participating in these programs provides hands-on experience and exposure to the racing industry, helping you refine your skills and gain recognition.

Getting more involved in the racing industry requires a proactive approach. Whether you're aiming to race professionally or simply want to immerse yourself in the sport, there are numerous ways to engage and make a meaningful impact. Pursue opportunities, build connections, and continue learning to enhance your involvement in the racing world.

Been involved in road racing can be incredibly rewarding, offering new perspectives and deeper connections within the community. Whether you're looking to volunteer, mentor, or even organize events, taking these steps will enrich your experience and allow you to give back to the sport you love.

11.　Glossary and Acronyms

Acronym	Meaning
ABS	Acrylonitrile-Butadiene-Styrene
AFFF	Aqueous Film Forming Foam
AWD	All Wheel Drive
BSI	British Standards Institute
CDS	Cold Drawn Steel
CFC	Chlorofluorocarbon
D.C.	Dielectric Constant
DOM	Drawn Over Mandrel
DOT	Department of Transportation
DT	Dilution Test
EBC	Electronic Boost Controller
ECE	Economic Commission for Europe
ECM	Engine Control Module
ECU	Electronic Control Unit
e.g.	Exempli Gratia; For Example
ERW	Electric Resistance Welded
EV	Electric Vehicle
FE	Fire Extinguishing
FIA	Fédération Internationale de l'Automobile
FT	Fuel Tank; Fuel Transfer
FTK	Fuel Tank
FWD	Front Wheel Drive
GT	Gran Turismo
HCFC	Hydrochlorofluorocarbon
HFC	Hydrofluorocarbon
HPDE	High-Performance Driving Event or Experience
HSR	Historic Sportscar Racing
IMSA	International Motor Sports Association
lbs.	Pounds
MAF	Mass Air Flow
NASA	National Auto Sport Association
N/A	Naturally Aspirated
NTH	Nice to have

Acronym	Meaning
OEM	Original Equipment Manufacturer
PCA	Porsche Club of America
Pro	Professional
PSI	Pound per Square Inch
PVC	Polyvinyl Chloride
RWD	Rear Wheel Drive
RV	Recreational Vehicle
SA	Snell Advanced Media
SA	Special Application
SCCA	Sport Club Car of America
SFI	Safety Foundation, Inc
SRO	Series Race Organizer
SS	Stainless Steel
ST	Street Touring
SVRA	Sportscar Vintage Racing Association
TA	Time Attack
Tech	Technical
TT	Time Trial

EPILOGUE

As you reach the end of this guide, it's clear that road racing is more than just a sport; it's a journey—a journey filled with passion, challenges, and personal growth. From the initial spark of curiosity that drives you to the track, to the meticulous planning of your budget, the choice of the perfect car, and the thrill of your first race, each step on this path is as crucial as the last.

The world of road racing is one where preparation meets opportunity, where skill is honed through relentless practice, and where community and camaraderie play as significant a role as speed and precision. Every lap around the track, every modification to your car, and every lesson learned from fellow racers contributes to your evolution as a driver and a participant in this exhilarating world.

But road racing is not just about the technical aspects or the adrenaline rush. It's about the stories you create along the way—the moments of triumph, the setbacks that teach you resilience, and the friendships forged in the heat of competition. It's about understanding that every race is not just against others, but against your own limitations, constantly pushing you to be better, faster, and more focused.

As you move forward, whether you're a novice or a seasoned racer, remember that the journey in road racing is ongoing. There's always another level to reach, another race to prepare for, and another challenge to overcome. Keep learning, keep growing, and most importantly, keep enjoying the ride. The road ahead is full of possibilities, and with the right mindset and preparation, you're well-equipped to navigate whatever comes your way.

So, strap in, fire up your engine, and get ready for the next chapter of your racing journey. The track is waiting, and the race is just beginning.